CZECH REPUBLIC

Travel Guide Book

A Comprehensive 5-Day Travel Guide to Prague,
Czech Republic & Unforgettable Czech Travel

• *Travel Guides to Europe Series* •

Passport to European Travel Guides

Eye on Life Publications

Prague, Czech Republic Travel Guide Book
Copyright © 2015 Passport to European Travel Guides

ISBN 10: 1519395671
ISBN 13: 978-1519395672

All rights reserved. No part of this book may be reproduced in any form or by any electronic or mechanical means, including information storage and retrieval systems, without permission in writing from the publisher, except by a reviewer who may quote brief passages in a review. All photos used courtesy of freeimages.com, HAAP Media Ltd., a subsidiary of Getty Images.

Other Travel Guide Books by Passport to European Travel Guides

Top 10 Travel Guide to Italy

Naples & the Amalfi Coast, Italy

Rome, Italy

Venice, Italy

Florence, Italy

Paris, France

Provence & the French Riviera, France

Top 10 Travel Guide to France

London, England

Barcelona, Spain

Amsterdam, Netherlands

Santorini, Greece

Greece & the Greek Islands

Berlin, Germany

Munich, Germany

Vienna, Austria

Istanbul, Turkey

Budapest, Hungary

Brussels, Belgium

"If European cities were a necklace, Prague would be a diamond among the pearls."
—Jean-Claude Adéméci

Table of Contents

Map of Prague, Czech Republic..................................7
Introduction: How to Use This Guide.........................9
City Snapshot...11
Before You Go...13
Getting in the Mood
  • What to Read...19
  • What to Watch...19

Local Tourist Information...21
About the Airports..21
How Long is the Flight?..22
Overview of Prague..23
★ Insider Tips for Tourists! ★..................................25
Czech Phrases For Emergencies...............................33
Climate and Best Times to Travel.............................36

Tours
  • Prague By Bike..39
  • Prague By Boat..40
  • Prague By Bus..40
  • Prague By Minibus or Car.................................41
  • Special Interest or Walking Tours.....................42

★ 5 Days in Prague—Itinerary! ★
  • Day 1...43
  • Day 2...46
  • Day 3...48
  • Day 4...51

- Day 5..52

Best Places For Travelers on a Budget
- Bargain Prague Sleeps......................................55
- Bargain Prague Eats..57

Best Places For Ultimate Luxury
- Luxury Prague Sleeps..59
- Luxury Prague Eats..60

Prague Nightlife
- Great Bars in Prague..63
- Great Clubs in Prague..64
- Great Live Music in Prague...............................65
- Great Theatre in Prague.....................................65

Conclusion..67

About the Authors...68

• Map of Prague •

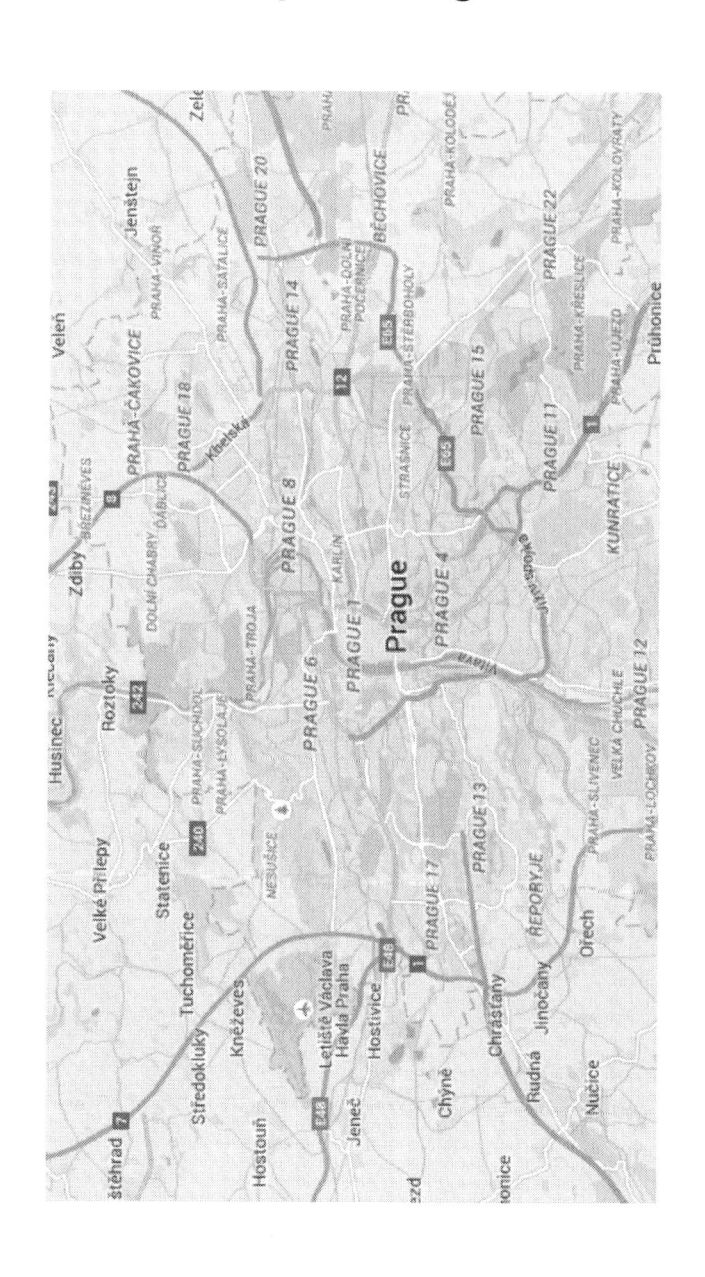

• Introduction •

Prague, Czech Republic. Located in central Europe, the city of Prague (Praha in Czech) rests exquisitely along the banks of the famed **Vltava River**.

Serenely nestled among some of the most beautiful rolling hills in the world, its **unparalleled sites** and **distinctive personality** mark Prague as one of **Europe's showcase capitals**.

As such, Prague has become a **must-see destination** when traveling through Europe. And although the Czech are **relatively reserved with foreigners** and nearly 100% of the residents speak Czech, don't worry; we've got you covered with all the necessary information you'll need to make this trip **a memorable success!**

In this 5-day guide to Prague, Czech Republic, you'll get the **sharpest recommendations** and **tips** to best prepare you with everything you need to know in order to have a most successful and memorable Czech experience!

Be sure to read over the **insider tips** carefully and familiarize yourself with the information so you can pack and prepare accordingly. **Every traveler is different**, so we've included a variety of information and recommendations to suit all interests. You can plan according to our detailed **5-day itinerary,** or you can **mix and match your activities** and scheduling to your own preferences. We encourage you to do whatever works for the enjoyment of your trip!

Enjoy!

The Passport to European Travel Guides Team

• City Snapshot •

Language: Czech

Local Airports: Václav Havel Airport Prague

Currency: Czech Koruna/Czech Crown (CZK)

Country Code: 420

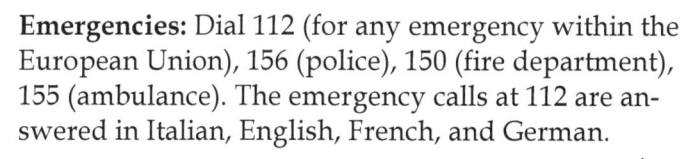

Emergencies: Dial 112 (for any emergency within the European Union), 156 (police), 150 (fire department), 155 (ambulance). The emergency calls at 112 are answered in Italian, English, French, and German.

• Before You Go... •

✓ Have a Passport

If you don't already have one, you'll need to apply for a passport in your home country a good two months before you intend to travel, to avoid cutting it too close. **You'll need to find a local passport agency**, complete an application, take fresh photos of yourself, have at least one form of ID and pay an application fee. **If you're in a hurry**, you can usually expedite the application for a 2-3 week turnaround at an additional cost.

✓ Need a Visa?

Residents of the US, Canada, Mexico and many other countries need not apply for a visa unless they are planning to spend more than 90 days in Prague. If you're unsure about your need for a visa, check the **city's website**. http://www.prague.com/v/visa_requirements

The US State Department provides a wealth of country-specific information for American travelers, including **travel alerts and warnings**, the location of the **US embassy in each country**, and of course, **whether or not you need a visa** to travel there!
http://travel.state.gov/content/passports/english/country.html

✓ Healthcare

Most people neglect this but it's important to keep in mind when traveling to any foreign country. It's wise to **consult with your doctor** about your travel plans and ensure routine immunizations are current. You want to protect against things like influenza, polio, chickenpox, mumps, measles, etc.

While healthcare is of the **highest quality** in Prague (and free for Czech citizens) foreigners must pay upfront for medical services, sometimes in part, but usually in full.

If you have **insurance at home**, be sure to check with them about **traveler's coverage**. It's important to know how you'll pay for services in case of an emergency while in Prague. **Give your insurance** information and passport at the time services are rendered, and **save receipts and bills** so your insurance company can reimburse you if appropriate.

✓ Set the Date

Choose the best time for the best experience! Unless you have no aversion to high expense and crowds of tourists, it's best to travel to Prague in the **off-season** — meaning avoid summer months. In **spring and autumn months**, the weather is milder and the crowds significantly fewer. Book flights, hotels and train passes **as far in advance** as possible, and you'll get better rates all around.

✓ Pack

• Since the **weather in Prague** tends to be on the cooler side (even in the summer), it's always a good idea to pack **sweaters, jackets, coats, long sleeves and pants**. **Unless it's wintertime**, you can also bring **shorts, cool shirts, dresses and skirts** for milder days. **Sunglasses, hats and sunscreen** are always a good idea, along with **an umbrella or raincoat** for when it rains. If you're traveling to **Prague in wintertime**, it'll be cold and snow is almost guaranteed, so pack layers.

• If you're planning on visiting any of the beautiful cathedrals of Prague, bring **clothes that appropriately cover** your shoulders and legs.

• Since this is a wonderful city to **explore on foot**, a comfortable pair of **walking shoes** or sneakers is highly recommended, especially for sightseeing tours.

• **A backpack** can be handy during the day when you go out sightseeing and collecting souvenirs, particularly when getting on and off buses, boats, trains or trams.

• Prague is a pretty casual city so most forms of attire are acceptable in restaurants, opera houses, concert halls and theatres.

• **If you don't speak Czech**, be sure to pack a good **conversational Czech phrase guide** to bring along with you. You'll find people a lot friendlier toward you if you don't go around assuming they speak your language.

- **Hand sanitizer** is always great to have along with you when traveling.

- A simple **first aid kit** is always a good idea to have in your luggage, just in case.

- **Medication.** Don't forget to have enough for the duration of your trip. It's also helpful to have a **note from your physician** if you're questioned for carrying a certain quantity.

- You can bring one or two **reusable shopping bags** for carrying souvenirs home.

- **Travelers from outside Europe** will need to bring along a **universal electrical plug converter** that can work for both lower and higher voltages. This way you'll be able to plug in your cell phones, tablets, curling irons, etc., during the trip.

- Be sure to **leave expensive jewels and high-priced electronics at home**. Like most major cities and tourist attractions, thieves and pickpockets abound. Avoid making yourself a target.

- **Take pictures of your travel documents and your passport** and email them to yourself before your trip. This can help in the unfortunate event they get lost or stolen.

- **Pack well,** but be sure to leave room for souvenirs!

✓ Phone Home

Consider how you will **call home** from Prague. Your cell phone company may offer service while abroad but be sure to consider the rates. **Calling cards** are also an option; they can be purchased at home or while in Prague.

✓ Currency Exchange

The Czech Crown is the form of currency used in Prague. Therefore, you will need to change your home currency to Czech Crowns. (Some hotels and restaurants accept euros, but most do not.) 1 Czech Crown is equivalent to approximately $24 USD but this changes daily. You can check the current exchange rate using this site:

http://finance.yahoo.com/currency-converter.

You'll almost always get a **better exchange rate** in Prague than at home. The easiest and most convenient method is to simply **withdraw cash at an airport ATM** once you land. Your bank may charge a transaction fee, so we recommend consulting them before you go so you know exactly how much it is.

It's always a good idea to **make sure your bank knows** you'll be traveling abroad. This way you avoid having foreign country transactions flagged and declined, which can be extremely inconvenient.

✓ Contact Your Embassy

In the unfortunate event you should lose your passport or be victimized while in Prague, **your country's embassy** will be able to help you. Be sure to give your itinerary and contact information to a **close friend or family member**, then also contact your embassy with your emergency contact information before you leave home.

✓ Your Mail

Ask a neighbor to check your mailbox while you're away, or visit your local post office and request a hold. **Overflowing mailboxes** are a dead giveaway that no one's home.

• Getting in the Mood •

Here are a few great book and film recommendations steeped in the **marvelous culture** of the Czech Republic!

What to Read:

We think you'll enjoy **The Joke by Milan Kundera** tells the story of an enthusiastic young Communist who uses his sarcastic sense of humor to change his odds and his life forever.

And how about **The Doctor Dines in Prague by Robin Hathaway,** a cozy, light-hearted mystery about a doctor who dashes off to Prague to discover foul play has befallen his dear cousin...

The Mercy Seller by Brenda Rickman Vantrease whisks you into the 15th century, where reading the bible for yourself constituted heresy!

What to Watch:

Loves of a Blonde (1966). A Czech New Wave classic, this story is a combination of sadness, unrequited love, and the frustrations of many single women who feel stuck in dead-end jobs.

Amadeus (1984). An Oscar-winning Mozart drama about the discovery of Amadeus's genius ability. Filmed partially in Prague.

Closely Watched Trains (1965). An Oscar-winning film that's considered a tragic comedy. A young man discovers his manhood during a resistance against the Nazis in World War II.

• Local Tourist Information •

The main tourist information centers are located in the Old Town:

Old Town Hall
Old Town Square, Prague 1 is open daily from 9:00 am – 7:00 pm.
Rytirska 31, Old Town, Prague 1:
Jan – March: Mon – Fri 10:00 am – 6:00 pm
Apr – Dec: Mon – Sat 10:00 am – 6:00 pm

Other tourist information centers are located at:

Prague Airport, Arrivals Hall
Terminal 1: Daily 9:00 am – 7:00 pm
Terminal 2: Daily 8:00 am – 8:00 pm

Wenceslas Square 42 (A kiosk near Stepanska Street)
New Town, Prague 1
Daily from 10:00 am – 6:00 pm

Lesser Town Bridge Tower
Lesser Town, Prague 1
Apr – Oct: Daily from 10:00 am – 6:00 pm

• About the Airports •

Václav Havel Airport Prague is a **modern and spacious** international airport. It's located on the northwest edge of Prague and about 12.5 miles north of the city. This is currently the only civil airport in Prague. http://www.prg.aero/en

• How Long is the Flight? •

- From **New York to Prague** = approx. 8.5 hours

- From **Chicago** = approx. 10 hours

- From **Miami** = approx. 11 hours

- From **Los Angeles** = approx. 14 hours

- From **London** = approx. 2 hours

- From **Sydney** = approx. 27 hours

- From **Cape Town** = approx. 15 hours

• Overview of Prague •

Under communism for over 40 years, tourists seldom visited the Czech Republic until 1989 when the world began to share in the **rich history** of this nation, which spans from the time of the **Holy Roman Empire** to the present day.

With its lush atmosphere and history, the city center of **Prague** is comprised of five independent towns and is considered to be one of the most attractive places on earth. **Magnificent art** and **mastery of architecture** shine brightly as signature mainstays.

As the capital of the Czech Republic, Prague has become one of the most popular city breaks in Europe. **With a history** dating back more than a thousand years, it's still a rather modern city, offering some of the best in **luxury hotel stays, excellent restaurants** and **dining, trendy nightclubs** and **elegant pubs**.

Famous sights include the **Charles Bridge**, **Old Town Square** and **Prague Castle**.

• Insider Tips for Tourists •

You'll find that **residents of Prague** are quite friendly and welcoming to visitors. And although most locals can speak and understand English, the primary language is Czech.

As a good visitor, we strongly urge you to learn a few words of the local language and to **keep your phrasebook handy**. By doing so, you'll always find people even more receptive and willing to help you.

Good phrases to learn are greetings, such as: **"dobrý den"** (doe-bree-dun) (good day), and goodbye: **"Dobrý večer"** (doe-bree-va-chair) (good evening).

Thank you is **"děkuji"** (dyeah-ko-yay). Excuse me is **"S dovolením"** (sss-duh-vol-neem).

Once upon a time, Prague was viewed as a reckless city, but this has changed. **Orderly conduct** is expected in public, **public intoxication** is not allowed and there are restrictions on smoking in public places.

Prague tourist guidebooks often use English names, but you'll find that **most maps and street signs** are in Czech. So we're including the following **Czech translations** for your convenience:

• Prague (Praha)
• Old Town (Staré Město)

- New Town (Nové Město)
- Charles Bridge (Karlův most)
- Prague Castle (Pražský Hrad)
- Wenceslas Square (Václavské náměstí)
- Old Town Square (Staroměstské náměstí)
- Lesser Town/Lesser Quarter/Lesser Side (Malá Strana)
- National Theatre translates (Národní divadlo)

Etiquette

- When approaching someone, it's always polite to first **let them know you don't speak Czech**: "**Nemluvím česky**" (neh-mul-vee-ne-chess-kay) (I don't speak Czech), and ask whether or not they speak English: "**Mluvite anglicky?**" (mul-vee-ta-angle-skay) (Do you speak English?).

- **Always offer greetings and goodbyes** when entering and leaving shops, elevators, restaurants, etc. It's considered **impolite** to walk into a store, etc., and not say hello and goodbye when you leave.

- **Handshaking** is common in casual meetings. Shake hello, shake goodbye. In business settings, **give your surname** while shaking the other person's hand.

Insider Tips For Tourists | 27

- Should you **visit someone's home or flat**, it's customary to **remove your outdoor shoes**. Some hosts may tell you not to bother, but it's still **good manners** to take them off. Most Czech homes keep **indoor shoes** for guess near the door.

- Unless you're in a **pub or club environment**, it's considered **rude to speak too loudly** in public.

Time Zone

There's a **six-hour time difference** between **New York and Prague** (Prague is ahead). When it's 8 am in New York it's 2 pm in Prague.

There's a **one-hour** time difference between **London and Prague** (Prague is ahead). When it's 8 am in London it's 9 am in Prague.

The format for abbreviating dates in Europe is different from the US. They use: **day/month/year**. So for example, August 23, 2019 is written in Prague as 23 August 2019, or 23/8/19.

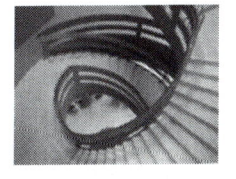

Saving Time & Money

The Prague Card is a sightseeing pass for tourists and can be purchased online at a **discounted price**: http://www.praguecard.com/index.php?lang=en, or once you arrive in Prague. With the Prague Card you can access 50 attractions and receive significant discounts on tickets to another 30+ attractions, including a free bus tour, river cruise and more.

It also gives unlimited use of the City Public Transport network for getting around. You will **save time**, as you won't have to stand in line for each sight, attraction or museum, and you'll **save money** on purchasing individual tickets for each attraction.

The Prague Card also comes with a free guide booklet (multi-lingual) packed with information on all of the city's attractions. The price of the card depends on the number of days you wish to spend sightseeing. Check the **Prague Card website** for **current pricing:** http://www.praguecard.com/index.php?lang=en

We also recommend purchasing one-day passes for public transportation, and **avoiding city center** hotels, restaurants, shops and nightclubs if you're on a budget.

Tipping

Tipping wasn't always commonplace in the Czech Republic, but today it's **expected of foreign visitors**, so it's a good idea to keep cash on-hand for tipping during your stay. Although the **Czech Crown** is the primary currency, both **euros and US dollars** are accepted in many businesses.

- If they provide excellent service, it's appropriate to tip **hotel concierges** about $20 USD.

- **Porters and bellboys** who assist with your luggage won't frown at $1 tip per bag.

- A small tip for **good housekeeping** if your stay is more than a night is acceptable as well.

- **In restaurants**, a service charge is usually included. If not, it's appropriate to leave a 10%-15% tip to your waiter or waitress. It's a general practice for you to pay the server directly for the total bill, including the tip.

- If you visit a **spa in Prague**, tip at least 10% for good service. You may tip the masseuse directly or leave it at the reception desk.

- You're also expected to tip **tour guides**, $15-$20 USD per person.

- Tipping for **taxi service** is not required in the Czech Republic, but if your driver's particularly helpful, you can round the fare up as a tip.

When You Have to Go

Public restrooms in Prague are usually labeled: "WC" and a small charge (approx. 5-10 CZK/0.50¢ USD) is required for use. You should find most of these **facilities clean** and regularly maintained.

You can find **free restrooms** available in many metro stations, department stores, museums, restaurants and cafés. It may be easier to use a free facility at fast food chains such as McDonalds or KFC, and in some museums and galleries.

Taxes

In Europe a **Value Added Tax (VAT)** is added to the majority of goods and services and should be incorporated in the advertised price. As of this writing, **VAT in the Czech Republic is 20%** for everything except certain items, such as food, books, newspapers and pharmaceuticals, which are 10%.

If you live outside of Europe, you can be reimbursed for private, non-commercial purchases that included VAT and exceed 2,000 CZK (about $80 USD). **For tourists**, VAT is refunded on purchases taken out of the country.

When you shop in locations bearing a "Tax Free Shopping" or "Tax Refund" logo, ask for a **stamped refund form + your receipt**. You will have up to **five months from the date of purchase** to present the form with your receipts to the custom's office at the Prague airport. If you're **traveling by train**, ask for the customs officer. The refund can be paid out in cash, as a credit on your credit card, or you can have a check mailed to your home address.

Important to note that items like food, gasoline, alcohol and cigarettes **are not eligible** for a tax refund.

You may also mail your information to one of the following refund agencies:

Global Blue Czech Republic
Address: Vodičkova 38/1935, 110 00 Praha 1, Czech Republic

Tel: +420 800 186 238
E-mail: info.cz@globalblue.com
http://www.globalblue.com/

Global Blue
Tel: 1-866-706-6090
E-mail: taxfree@global-blue.com
www.global-blue.com

Premier Tax Free
Tel: +420 222 250 263
E-mail: info@cz.premiertaxfree.com
www.premiertaxfree.com

Phone Calls

The country code for Prague is 420. When calling Prague from outside the country, you **drop the first 0** from the number, then dial the international access prefix, then 420 followed by the nine-digit Czech number.

When calling home from Prague, first dial 00 and after you hear a dial tone, dial the country code, the area code **without the initial 0,** and then the number.

To reach an **International Operator** dial: 133004. For **International Directory Assistance** dial: 1181.

It can be expensive to call internationally **from a hotel** phone as they assess **heavy surcharges**. Therefore, buying a calling card may be your best bet for staying in touch in a cost-efficient way. There's also Skype,

Google Talk, and free texting services like WhatsApp to **stay in touch without cost**.

Calling cards are available at many money-changing stands and will work with any phone once you enter a 14-digit code.

Electricity

The electrical current in Prague is **230 volts** (for comparison, the US uses 120 volts), with standard European **two-prong plugs**. As previously mentioned, when traveling from outside Europe, you will need to bring an **adapter and converter** that will enable you to plug your electronics and appliances into the sockets. Cell phones, tablets and laptop chargers are typically dual voltage so you may not need a converter, just an adapter. If you don't have one and forget to pick one up in the airport, adaptors are readily available in Prague.

In Emergencies

In Prague, the number for emergencies is not 911. So don't bother dialing it, it won't work. The numbers for emergencies are as follows:

- **General Emergency** — Dial 112
- **Fire** — 150
- **Medical Emergency** — 155
- **Prague City Police** — 156

Czech Phrases for Emergencies:

• Help! = Pomoc!
• Fire! = Hoří!
• Thief! = Zloděj!
• Call an ambulance / a doctor! = Zavolejte sanitku / doktora!
• Call the police! = Zavolejte policii!
• Where is the police station? = Kde je policejní stanice?
• My purse / bag has been stolen = Ukradli mi kabelku / tašku.
• I have been robbed = Byl jsem okraden.
• I have lost my passport / bag = Ztratil jsem pas / tašku.
• I want to call my embassy = Chci si zavolat na ambasádu.

There are **24-hour pharmacies** available in the city, most in the New Town area. Your hotel should be able to direct you to the nearest one. In Prague, even over-the-counter medication needs to be purchased at a pharmacy.

Doctors who offer **24-hour tourist services** can be found at the following:

Health Centre Prague International Clinic
Address: Vodickova 28, 110 00, Praha, Czech Republic — 3rd entrance, 2nd floor
Tel: +420 224 220 040
The 24-hour emergency number is: +420 603 433 833

It is not uncommon to encounter closed doors rather than an open nursing station, so you may need to **knock or ring for service**.

Holidays

Prague has **twelve public holidays** to keep in mind when planning your vacation. You may find that when a holiday falls on a Tuesday or Thursday a lot of businesses are closed on that Monday and Friday as well.

Listed below are the **public holidays in the Czech Republic.** Check for the specific dates in if traveling during the Easter holiday, as the date fluctuates each year:

January 1 (New Year's Day)
March/April (Easter Monday)
May 1 (Labour Day)
May 8 (Liberation Day)
July 5 (Saints Cyril and Methodius Day)

July 6 (Jan Hus Day)
September 28 (St. Wenceslas Day)
October 28 (Independent Czechoslovak State Day)
November 17 (Struggle for Freedom and Democracy Day)
December 24 (Christmas Eve)
December 25 (Christmas Day)
December 26 (St. Stephen's Day)

Hours of Operation

Bank hours in Prague are typically Monday – Friday from 9:00 am to 5:00 pm.

Shopping centers and department stores open between 8:00 am and 9:00 am and close from 8:00 pm – 10:00 pm.

Small shops open as early as 7:00 am – 08:00 am and close at 6:00 pm – 7:00 pm.

Convenience stores are usually open until 10:00 pm or 11:00 pm, although prices may be higher.

Many shops, including shopping centers and department stores are usually open on Sunday as well.

Climate & Best Time to Travel

Most tourists visit Prague during the **summer months (June, July, August)**. Although the weather may be relatively warm, many enjoy the euphoria created by the summer holidays. Average temperature is **mid-70s** in the summertime.

Spring and **autumn** are nice times to visit, when the temperatures are cool, averaging **mid-50s**. It's also a great time to mingle with the locals who have beer parties behind their houses. Fall in particular is a **quieter time** to visit Prague, as there are **fewer tourists**. So if you prefer fewer crowds, these are the months for you.

Winters can see snow and temperatures in the **mid to low 30s**. Not ideal for sightseeing, but it's certainly the **least expensive** time to travel to Prague. You'll find the **best rates at hotels** and the **best airfares**.

Transportation

Good transportation can make or break any vacation plan. **With metros, trams and buses,** you can rest assured that Prague has one of the **best public transportation** systems in all of Europe.

We highly recommend utilizing public transportation instead of taking cabs or renting cars. Traffic has become increasingly dense in the city center and no visitor wants to spend most of his or her time waiting around in the gridlock.

The Prague Airport Shuttle service is relatively inexpensive and can get you to the center of the city in a matter of minutes if that's where you're staying. There are also **buses** available outside the terminals:
http://www.prague-airport-shuttle.cz

Even less expensive options are the **metro train and tram system** that serves the entire city. You can purchase passes for daily use, or one-way.

In some places, **walking** may be the best option. Like if you plan to visit the Old Town area, your feet can serve you quite well.

Biking is also an option, but we don't recommend it for anyone who isn't familiar with the area; the city streets can be very narrow.

Driving

As a tourist, it's best to **avoid driving** in Prague unless you're already familiar with the area, or plan to leave the city and explore the countryside. The city's cobblestoned roadways are narrow and often congested.

If you do decide to rent a car, make sure you have a **working GPS** in English. Your home driver's license will be sufficient so long as you plan to be in Prague for **less than 60 days**. If your stay will be longer, you'll need to get a Czech license. **Seat belts** are mandatory and **alcohol in the blood stream is prohibited.**

Also, we recommend **going with a well-known brand name rental company,** as the airport is full of shady car rental outfits.

• Tours •

If your **time in Prague is limited** or you'd just like to make the most of it and have trouble speaking and understanding the Czech language, **guided tours** are a great option for getting the most out of your vacation.

Check the provided websites for the most current rates, schedules and meeting places. We recommend making sure you're clear on all fees and taxes that may be included in the prices so there are no surprises. Also, remember to carry some cash to **tip the tour guide(s)** at the end.

Prague By Bike

City Bike Prague is the original bike tour company in Prague and our top recommendation. You can enjoy one of their guided group tours, or you can rent a bike for a self-guided tour. Either way, photo-ops abound!

City Bike Prague
Address: Králodvorská 667/5, 110 00, Praha, Czech Republic
Tel: +420 776 180 284
http://www.citybike-prague.com

Prague By Boat

For a truly great experience on the water, **Prague Boats** is one of the best options. They have a very modern fleet and a good variety of boating options.

Prague Boats
Address: Dvořákovo nábř., 110 00 Praha 1, Czech Republic
Tel: +420 224 810 030
http://www.prague-boats.cz/

For a classic boat tour experience, we recommend a sightseeing boat tour with **Prague Experience.** Upgrade options are available to include lunch, dinner, and jazz boat tours.

Prague Experience
Address: Krizovnicke Namesti 3, Old Town, Prague 1, Prague, Czech Republic
Tel: +420 168 989 8500
http://www.pragueexperience.com

Prague By Bus

For a nice bus tour experience of the city, we suggest **HopON-HopOFF**. There are a plethora of options, and buses depart every 45 minutes from eight different locations near the city's main attractions. Depending on where you're staying, shuttles can even pick you up from your hotel. Book online for a discounted rate.

HopON-HopOFF
Address: Jindřišská 24, 110 00 Praha 1, Czech Republic
Tel: +420 602 405 701
http://www.hopon-hopoff.cz

Prague By Minibus or Car

You can also opt for a minibus or car tour of Prague. These tours are great for larger families, social groups or for those looking for more private and intimate tour experience. **Private Prague Guide Custom Travel Services** offers economical tours with a variety of options for an enhanced experience.

Private Prague Guide Custom Travel Services
Address: Custom Travel Services s.r.o. (Ltd), Blanická 922/25, 120 00 Praha 2, Czech Republic
Tel: +420 773 103 102
https://www.private-prague-guide.com

Or you could **treat yourself** a bit and indulge in an antique car tour with **Prague Private Guides!**

Prague Private Guides
Tel: +420 222 518 259
http://www.guidingprague.com/en/home-prague-tours

Try Special Interest and Walking Tours

There are a variety of walking tours to choose from in Prague, but our favorite is with **Sandemans New Europe Prague.** The guides offer a wonderful, interactive, upbeat and knowledgeable time.

They offer daily tours, rain or shine. Reservations are best, but walk-ups are also welcome.

Sandemans New Europe Prague
Address: Prague 160 00, Czech Republic
Tel: +420 222 317 229
http://www.newpraguetours.com

Want to explore the **Jewish side of Prague?** Perhaps you're someone who's passionate about **architecture, stunning art, literature, food, music, or the Cold War?** Well, just see the **Prague Travel Concierge!** Book a once in a lifetime **specialized tour experience** — we can't recommend it highly enough!

Prague Travel Concierge
Address: Vysehradska 47, Prague, 12800, Czech Republic
Tel: +420 603 250 200
http://praguetravelconcierge.com

• 5 Days in Prague! •

Please enjoy this 5-day itinerary for a well-balanced and memorable experience of Prague! Modify or adjust if you like, we have several options given in the **upcoming sections** on budget and luxury hotel recommendations, and for enjoying Prague's nightlife and theater — and always keep in mind that it's best to buy your tickets and make reservations ahead of time whenever possible. **Check websites** and/or **call** for the current rates and hours of operation. Enjoy!

• Day 1 •

It's best to arrive in Prague in the morning whenever possible. Once you check into your hotel or arrive at the place you're staying, relax and freshen up a bit before heading back out. This is always a good time to get to know Prague.

Hungry? Take a stroll over to **Wenceslas Square** (Václavské náměstí) in New Town. There are lots of great restaurants in this part of town. We like **Como Restaurant** and think you will too. Their Mediterranean fare is delicious.

Next, take a walk across the **Charles Bridge**, one of Prague's most photographed attractions. Follow the bridge to the Castle side of the river—this part of town will leave you in awe. The walk to **Prague Castle** should take about 40 minutes, then you'll see: The famous **St. Vitus Cathedral, the Powder Tower, St. George's Basilica, and the Old Royal Palace**.

You can spend a few hours sightseeing here before heading back to your hotel for dinner and a good night's rest. Day Two awaits!

Location Information:

Wenceslas Square
Location: 110 00 Prague 1, Czech Republic

Como Restaurant (& Cafe)
Address: Václavské nám. 818/45, 110 00 Praha 1, Czech Republic
Tel: +420 222 247 240
http://www.comorestaurant.cz

Charles Bridge
Location: Karlův most, 110 00 Praha 1, Czech Republic

Prague Castle/St. George's Basillica
Address: 119 08 Prague 1, Czech Republic
Tel: +420 224 373 368
http://www.hrad.cz/en/index.shtml

Powder Tower
Location: nám. Republiky 5, 110 00 Praha 1, Czech Republic

Old Royal Palace
Address: Hrad III. nádvoří, 110 00 Prague, Czech Republic
Tel: +420 224 373 584

St. Vitus Cathedral
Address: III. nádvoří 48/2, 119 01 Praha 1, Czech Republic
Tel: +420 224 372 434
https://www.katedralasvatehovita.cz/en

• Day 2 •

After enjoying a nice breakfast in your hotel or at nearby cafe, the **perfect day trip** awaits you!

Karlovy Vary (Carlsbad) is about two hours from Prague by car or bus. Known as a picturesque spa town, the healing waters of Karlovy Vary has hosted many over the years, including Beethoven and Chopin!

Prague Experience offers a wonderful Karlovy Vary Sightseeing and Moser Glass Tour:

http://www.pragueexperience.com/places.asp?PlaceID=643

If you choose to take the **guided tour,** you'll be dropped off near Wenceslas Square when you get back. We recommend dining at **KOBE Restaurant** where they serve delicious international cuisine and live jazz on weekends.

After dinner, if you're not too tired from the bus ride and still have some pep in your step, **a beer** before settling in is always nice. Prague's wide variety of beer choices is lauded as some of the best in Europe, yet relatively inexpensive. Most pubs serve their own **signature flavors**.

So for tasty food, a friendly atmosphere and an opportunity to enjoy beer in Prague Old Town, visit **U Kunštátů.**, a local beer garden with beer tastings every evening at 6:00 pm. Then you can **head back to your hotel** and get a good night's rest; it's undoubtedly been quite a long day!

Location Information:

KOBE
Address: Vaclavske Namesti 11, Prague 110 00, Czech Republic
Tel: +420 224 267 248
http://www.koberestaurant.cz/en

U Kunštátů
Address: Řetězová 3, 110 00 Praha 1, Czech Republic
Tel: +420 601 353 776
http://ukunstatu.cz

• Day 3 •

Today may be a good day to spend in **Prague Old Town**. The narrow streets can lead you to every sort of **souvenir shop** imaginable.

Enjoy the abundant craftsmanship. Shop for **puppets or marionettes**, staples of Czech culture since the 1500s. We recommend taking the time to shop around, as they can be quite expensive.

In the afternoon, how about lunch at **U Kroka?** Followed by a visit to the well known **Jewish Quarter?** See the houses, synagogues, the famous cemetery and the **Jewish Museum**. The museum treasures were curated by none other than Adolph Hitler. He had intended the exhibit for posterity, to memorialize an extinct race.

The Jewish Quarter is located between the Old Town Square and the Vltava River. You can arrange a walking tour via **Prague Experience**.

Should your spirits need lifting after the museum tour, check out the **Prague Astronomical Clock at the Old Town City Hall**. The breathtaking views of the city makes climbing to the top more than worth it!

Since you're in Old Town, have dinner at the **Field Restaurant**. They serve some of the most **divine international and Czech cuisine** and are touted as the best in the area.

Tonight, you can take in a **classical concert**. See our top recommendations for great theater in Prague ahead!

Location Information:

Prague Old Town Square
Location: Staroměstské nám., 110 00 Praha 1, Czech Republic

U Kroka
Address: Vratislavova 12, 128 00 Praha 2 - Vyšehrad, Czech Republic
Tel: +420 775 905 022
http://www.ukroka.cz/ - !home/c402

The Jewish Quarter (Josefov)
Location: Josefov, Prague 1, Czech Republic

The Jewish Museum
Address: U staré školy 141/1, 110 00 Praha 1, Czech Republic
Tel: +420 222 749 211
http://www.jewishmuseum.cz/en/info/visit

Prague Astronomical Clock
Location: Staroměstské nám. 1, 110 00 Praha 1, Czech Republic
Tel: +420 236 002 629
http://www.staromestskaradnicepraha.cz/en

Field Restaurant
Address: U milosrdných 12, 110 00 Praha 1-Staré Město, Czech Republic

Tel: +420 222 316 999
http://www.fieldrestaurant.cz/en/

• Day 4 •

Relax this morning. Sleep in. Enjoy a fresh cup of coffee with breakfast. When you're ready for more of what Prague has to offer, hop aboard a ferry for a cruise along the **River Vltava**.

One option for cruising on the River Vltave is to purchase a **Prague Lunch River Cruise** through **Prague Experience**. Their cruises include a bar, live music and a tasty three-course hot and cold buffet dinners: http://www.pragueexperience.com/places.asp?PlaceID=647

After the cruise, you can enjoy a relaxing afternoon in the park. **Letenské Sady** (Letná Park) is one of several beautifully serene parks in Prague, located on Letná Hill just across the **Cechuv Bridge**.

We highly recommend stopping in the **Bombay Bar** over in Old Town Square tonight for good eats, lively music and a great cocktail bar atmosphere. After eating, you can make the most of the dance floor and have a really good time!

Location Information:

Letná Park
Location: 170 00 Prague, Czech Republic

Bombay Bar
Address: Dlouhá 13, 110 00 Praha 1, Czech Republic
Tel: +420 222 324 040
http://www.bombay-bar.cz/en

• Day 5 •

Today is the perfect day to check out some of the spots you may have wanted to see but haven't gotten to. Perhaps go see **"Fred and Ginger,"** the infamous **Dancing Building?** Who can skip seeing this marvel of modern architecture up close?

You might consider **revisiting the New Town** district. If the mood strikes you, **splurge on yourself today** and enjoy some **unstructured time** with the city. Alternatively, you could **book another sightseeing tour** or revisit a **favorite spot**.

While in New Town, we think you might enjoy a delicious BBQ dinner in the garden. **Le Grill Restaurant** is located in **The Mark Luxury Hotel** and serves amazing international, barbecue and authentic Czech cuisine — it's one of our favorites in Prague!

After dinner, you could check out a popular pub that has at least **twenty different taps** and a nice garden out back — the wonderful **Prague Beer Museum**.

Location Information:

Dancing Building
Address: Jiráskovo náměstí 1981/6, 120 00 Praha 2, Czech Republic
Tel: +420 605 083 611
http://www.tancici-dum.cz/index.php?lg=en

New Town Prague
Location: 120 00 Prague 2, Czech Republic

Le Grill Restaurant
Address: Hybernska 12 | The Mark Luxury Hotel Prague, Prague 110 00, Czech Republic
Tel: +420 226 226 126
http://en.themark.cz/restaurant-le-grill

Prague Beer Museum
Address: Dlouhá 720/46, 110 00 Praha 1-Staré Město, Czech Republic
Tel: +420 732 330 912
http://www.praguebeermuseum.com/en

• Best Places for Travelers on a Budget •

With a few tips and proper planning you can explore the **budget-friendly** options Prague has to offer. You may well be pleasantly surprised what you find!

• Bargain Prague Sleeps

Pension Brezina is in a good location, a close walk to tram and subway links and just a short walk from Charles Bridge, Wenceslas Square and the Old City. The rooms are simple but clean and affordable. You should find the staff polite and very helpful to tourists.

Address: Legerova 39-41, 120 00 Praha 2, Czech Republic
Tel: +420 224 266 779
http://www.brezina.cz

EA Hotel Jasmín is a 3-star hotel that's a little bit further from the city but very affordable. The hotel staff is also friendly, but all may not speak the best English. The rooms are spacious and well kept and the hotel promotes a peaceful environment. Breakfast is complimentary.

Address: U Kloubových domů 515/3, 190 00, Czech Republic
Tel: +420 271 090 832
http://www.hoteljasminprague.cz/en

If you're traveling in a group, we recommend **Your Apartments.** You can book a vacation apartment and **spend quite a bit less** than if you all stayed in a hotel. Just a 15-minute walk from the city, an apartment is not only cost-efficient, but well kept and equipped with full kitchens and TV areas.

Address: Národní 1987/22, 110 00, Prague 1, Czech Republic
Tel: +420 773 914 566
http://www.yourapartments.com

Mosaic House is a great **hostel** near New Town we highly recommend — good rooms, showers, breakfast, bar, lounge and activities.

Address: Odborů 4, 120 00 Praha 2, Czech Republic
Tel: +420 228 883 351
https://www.mosaichouse.com/en

• Bargain Prague Eats

CzecHouse Grill & Rotisserie is a budget friendly eatery that serves American, Czech and European cuisine. It's a great value that shouldn't blow your budget to smithereens!

Address: Pobřežní 1, Florenc, 186 00 Praha, Czech Republic
Tel: +420 224 842 700
http://www.hiltonprague.com/prague-dining/restaurants-en.html

Butcher's Grill & Pasta is another affordable eatery that serves American food, steak, hamburgers and good pasta; it has a very nice atmosphere as well. Reservations are recommended but not necessary.

Address: Dobrovského 29, 612 00 Brno, Czech Republic
Tel: +420 605 262 659
http://www.butchers.cz/en

The Pastar Restaurant and Food Shop has affordable pricing and serves a nice variety of international dishes with an inviting décor. They also have a reasonable wine bar. Reservations are recommended but not necessary.

Address: Malostranske Nabrezi 1, Prague 101 00, Czech Republic
Tel: +420 777 009 108
http://www.pastar.cz

• Best Places for Ultimate Luxury •

• Luxury Prague Sleeps

Our top recommendation is definitely **Pachtuv Palace,** a 5-star hotel we know you'd love. Located in the heart of Prague, it's the closest hotel to Charles Bridge. If you want a little romance while you're in Prague, this is the hotel for you! **Rooms and suites are stunning** and designed to make your stay luxuriously unforgettable.

Address: Karolíny Světlé 34, 110 00 Praha 1, Czech Republic
Tel: +420 234 705 111
http://pachtuvpalace.com

Design Hotel Jewel Prague is a luxury hotel **just a short walk** from many of Prague's star attractions. The tasty breakfast buffet, the choice of fragrance for your room, your choice of pillows, bath robes, quality toiletries and a **beautiful décor** are just some of the features that sets this hotel apart from its competitors. We think you'd really like it here!

Address: Rytířská 3, 110 00 Praha-Staré Město, Czech Republic
Tel: +420 224 211 699
http://hoteljewelprague.com

Hotel Liberty is one of the highest rated hotels in the Czech Republic. Located in Prague's historical center and near the famous Wenceslas Square, this one offers **all the comfort and amenities** sought in opulent accommodations.

Address: 28. Října 376/11, 110 00 Praha 1, Czech Republic
Tel: +420 224 239 598
https://www.hotelliberty.cz

• Luxury Prague Eats

Chilli Point, known to be one of the top restaurants in Prague, serves some of the best international fare. Meals are all **beautifully prepared and presented,** with a taste that's just as lovely. The atmosphere is **cozy and inviting** and lends itself to a very pleasant dining experience. Reservations are not necessary, but still recommended.

Address: Havelska 8, Prague 110 00, Czech Republic
Tel: +420 224 248 606
http://www.chillipoint.cz

George Prime Steak is known for serving up the best steak meal in Prague, a great restaurant to visit on **special occasions or romantic getaways** in Prague. Before you place your order the staff presents you with **different cuts of beef** to choose from. From tip to tail your dining experience will be exemplary, as the ambiance, service and the food are all marvelous here.

Address: Platnéřská 111/19, 110 00 Praha 1, Czech Republic
Tel: +420 226 202 599
http://georgeprimesteak.com

Alcron is known for providing customers with an ultimate gourmet experience. Meals include international fare, European and Czech. You dine in an **art deco décor** with meals that are sure to exceed your expectations in presentation and taste. Reservations are available but not necessary.

Address: Štěpánská 624/40, 110 00 Praha 1-Nové Město, Czech Republic
Tel: +420 222 820 410
http://www.alcron.cz

Terasa U Zlaté Studně restaurant is not only known for providing a most spectacular dining experience, but also for a breathtaking view overlooking the city. Dining options include breakfast, lunch, dinner, dessert, late night and even delivery. Reservations are available but not required.

Address: U Zlaté studně 166/4, 118 00 Praha 1, Czech Republic

Tel: +420 257 533 322
http://www.terasauzlatestudne.cz/en

• Prague Nightlife •

Nightlife in Prague is a lively, enriching experience. When the sun goes down, the city offers good music, friendly locals and small bakeries on the street corners for late night snacks. It's always a great time to **enjoy Prague city life!**

• Great Bars in Prague

Cloud 9 Sky Bar & Lounge was the first sky bar in Prague. Atop the Hilton Hotel, you can see the most **breathtaking panoramic views** through its cool glass interior. They specialize in innovative food concepts and **original cocktails**. Definitely hang out here at least once!

Address: Hilton Prague Hotel, Pobřežní 1, 186 00 Praha 8, Czech Republic
Tel: +420 224 842 999

http://www.cloud9.cz

The Bed Lounge may surprise you...because that's *exactly* what it is! It was the first ever "bed" restaurant and bar opened in Prague. Looking to relax on a **stylish bed?** Or chill at a trendy table enjoying delicious international cuisine with a large variety of unique cocktails to choose from? **Visit the Bed Lounge!**

Address: Dlouhá 2, 110 00, Czech Republic
Tel: +429 222 314 358
http://www.bedlounge.cz

• Great Clubs in Prague

If you wouldn't mind experiencing "Hawaii" while in Prague, the **Aloha Wave Lounge** is the spot for you! With an old-fashioned Hawaiian tiki bar décor, Aloha is known for its friendly atmosphere, modern cuisine and wide range of exotic cocktails. But you won't just sit drinking for too long — the dance floor awaits!

Address: Dušní 11, 110 00 Praha 1, Czech Republic
Tel: +420 602 251 392
http://alohapraha.cz/en

Located in the Fusion Hotel Prague, the **360° Lounge Bar** has the honor of being known as Europe's first **revolving bar**. The art deco atmosphere and **circular glass roof** allows for both a relaxing drink and the opportunity to let loose on the dance floor with the rest of the party.

Address: Panska 9, Prague, Czech Republic
Tel: +420 226 222 996
http://www.360loungeandbar.cz

• Great Live Music in Prague

If you visit Prague in the springtime, definitely get to the **Spring International Music Festival**. This is a yearly event featuring music concerts in the various concert halls throughout the city. Check their website for current dates and line-ups:
http://www.festival.cz/en

The **Prague Castle** serves as a location for several live musical performances throughout the year. Visit the Castle's website for current bookings.

Address: 119 08 Prague 1, Czech Republic
Tel: +420 224 373 368
http://www.hrad.cz/en/index.shtml

• Great Theatre in Prague

The **National Theatre** serves as the ultimate stage in the Czech Republic. Opening for the first time in 1881, the Theatre was built with monies received from a nationwide collection. The atmosphere created by the **richly embellished gold interior** enhances the theatergoing experience. Performances include drama, ballet and opera. Visit the website for upcoming performances.

Address: Národní 2, 110 00 Praha 1, Czech Republic
Tel: +420 224 901 448
http://www.narodni-divadlo.cz/en

Mozart himself performed at the **Prague Opera Estates Theatre!** Need we say more?

Address: Železná ulice / Ovocný trh, Praha 1, Czech Republic
Tel: +420 224 901 448
http://www.estatestheatre.cz

The O2 Arena, one of the most modern arenas in Europe, is a **multi-function arena** with the capacity to seat 18,000 occupants. Annually, the O2 arena welcomes over 600,000 visitors for sporting, cultural and musical events. **World-renowned superstars** perform here regularly, so you'll want to check the website for upcoming performances—they could help you **choose the dates** for your getaway to Prague!

Address: Českomoravská 2345/17, 190 00 Praha 9, Czech Republic
Tel: +420 266 771 000
http://www.o2arena.cz

• Conclusion •

We hope you have found our guide to **the amazing city of Prague**, helpful. It was created in the interest of enhancing and preparing you for an **unforgettable experience**, and helping you make the most of the time you spend in Prague.

We wish you a **safe, happy and fun-filled** trip to Prague!

Warm regards,

The Passport to European Travel Guides Team

Visit our Blog!

http://www.passporttoeuropeantravelguides.blogspot.com

★ **Join our mailing list** ★ to follow our Travel Guide Series. You'll be automatically entered for a chance to win a **$100 Visa Gift Card** in our monthly drawings! Be sure to respond to the confirmation e-mail to complete the subscription.

• **About the Authors** •

PASSPORT TO European Travel
The Best Travel Guides to Europe!

Passport to European Travel Guides is an eclectic team of international jet setters who know exactly what travelers and tourists want in a cut-to-the-chase, comprehensive travel guide that suits a wide range of budgets.

Our growing collection of distinguished European travel guides are guaranteed to give first-hand insight to each locale, complete with day-to-day, guided itineraries you won't want to miss!

We want our brand to be your official Passport to European Travel — one you can always count on!

Bon Voyage!

The Passport to European Travel Guides Team
http://www.passporttoeuropeantravelguides.blogspot.com

Monuments   Jakub Arbes
Taras Shevchenko

Trip Advisor
Alelier Red & Wine duck near hotel
Art & Food - quirky near hotel
Paston Italian on river dessert

Must Do

Hunger Wall   Petrin Hill
Petrin Hill - tower - tram - view - park
Prague Welcome Card 34.33

Kampa Park Art - canals

John Lennon Wall —
    near Kampa Island & Park

Dancing Building Old Townside
    Jiraskovo namEsti 1981
    on other side of Vltava River
    use Jiraskovo most (bridge)

Kostel Panny Astronomical Clock - light show?
Marie Church free evening concert
    Charles Bridge

    St Vitus Cathedral in Castle
        District near Charles Bridge
        Matel side &

    Lobkowicz Palace - Mozart
                          concert
    Kostel Panny Marie Pnd Tynen
        inspired Walt Disney, free evening
                                      concert

State Opera pr National Theater

Walking Tour
Prague Walking Tour Following
in Mozart Footsteps Eva Pyp 20

Made in the USA
Lexington, KY
31 August 2016